About the Author

Alexa (Lexi) Lewis is a twenty-seven-year-old American writer who was born and raised in a small town in West Virginia. She is a single mother of a five-year-old son, a second time publishing author after self-publishing *Four Letters* in 2019, an avid outdoors seeker, and nature lover, especially of marine life.

Write the Letters

L. Lewis

Write the Letters

Olympia Publishers
London

www.olympiapublishers.com
OLYMPIA PAPERBACK EDITION

Copyright © L. Lewis 2023

The right of L. Lewis to be identified as author of
this work has been asserted in accordance with sections 77 and 78 of
the Copyright, Designs and Patents Act 1988.

All Rights Reserved

No reproduction, copy or transmission of this publication
may be made without written permission.
No paragraph of this publication may be reproduced,
copied or transmitted save with the written permission of the publisher,
or in accordance with the provisions
of the Copyright Act 1956 (as amended).

Any person who commits any unauthorized act in relation to
this publication may be liable to criminal
prosecution and civil claims for damage.

A CIP catalogue record for this title is
available from the British Library.

ISBN: 978-1-80439-046-7

This is a work of fiction.
Names, characters, places and incidents originate from the writer's
imagination. Any resemblance to actual persons, living or dead, is
purely coincidental.

First Published in 2023

Olympia Publishers
Tallis House
2 Tallis Street
London
EC4Y 0AB

Printed in Great Britain

Dedication

I dedicate this book to my son, Ezra Wolfe Lewis. Thank you for growing with me when I was just a kid myself when you came into this world. I love you, always. To my grandfather, my sweet papaw, thank you for always believing in me. I miss you more than I have words for and love you endlessly. All my love, always…
Lex.

Acknowledgements

To my best friend, my person, Andrea. Thank you for being here through it all with me. For loving me and supporting me more than anyone ever has. I love you.

I had my fair share of being second choice.
Not always by another lover, but by simple life. The barriers it can create between two hearts if you let it.
Time slipped through your fingers faster than you could catch it within its fall.
Materialism found its way inside the space I once held.
It's disheartening, the way you watch as the outside world finds its way into the purest of pieces that once held space only for you.
But instead of purity to refill that space, they fill it with reckless things.
And each day, I felt the closing of the walls in a place I once thought to be home, and suddenly, I couldn't breathe.
Instead of closing the door, I watched from a different view.
I watched as the world took every ounce, every piece of what I knew, that was you
— yet hollow

I have seen the harshest of soul's damn love, and all that it is.
But that's how I know it's real.
Because had they not felt love
they wouldn't despise it for its counterpoint.

I swallowed the hours.
That seeped from you, thirsty for your words.

Who are you hoping to read your story and feels it beneath their skin?
The ones who have felt my absence

I wish I could tell you just how many times the word "safe," ruined new beginnings for me.
I would rather stand in front of failure and soak in its lessons than hide behind fear and what could have been, and what could be.

I am not where you left me, my palms you left empty.
You may fool the ones who haven't seen your naked soul like I have.
But I, have tasted more of your love, seen your soul stripped bare, watched temptation drip down your lips to your tongue that swallowed a regret that never came.
You will begin again.
And you will realize
you were looking into the wrong eyes all along.
"You are trying to control a heart, that is living beyond, right now. Instead of realizing you were given today."
Ten. "Do you not fall, bored and restless, living day to day without knowing?"
He said with a smirk
I smiled in return,
"And do you not feel empty knowing your day to day without risking, because you fear not knowing the unknown?"
Outgrown

I grew tired of being your what if while you were my only.

Play me like a violin,
feeling your touch along my porcelain skin. Explore me, like the newness of a place you've never been.
Chaotic, taking up space inside your addictive soul.
Losing to a love, that you can no longer control.

Like a book with missing pages and a story left untold,
of ending that never came the one where we grew old.

Wandering saved my soul. It was the illusion of security that began to ruin me.
So I left

"Tell me of love," he said.
Isn't it strange how we always see another when we think of love? We see them, standing there at one twenty-five a.m. with their back against the doorframe. Sweatpants that have stains of old white paint splattered on the legs.
Holding a bowl of ice cream, smiling behind the spoon while shaking their head at their own jokes.
"Love is ever changing. But you learn to grow with it. You learn with time, that love and lust aren't weaved into the same pattern. One will find its way into your veins, and the other merely fades into someone new without a second thought.
It's forgetting when you first said those eight letters, but you remember exactly where you were standing when it rolled off your tongue. You remember the way his hands felt when they found your face, the way he smelled like spearmint as he leaned in to put his forehead to yours.
You will remember the way they look at seven a.m. Hair a mess, eyes swollen, a half-smile to greet you without words.
Love is simply a word to use when there are too many other words to describe what another soul can do to you, if you let them in.
It's growing. It's changing. It's remembering moments that you never thought you'd miss, until you feel their absence."

"Keep going.
You'll break again,
but love, I promise
you will you be much more balanced.
Every time.
But that's just how this goes, so find your footing again.
You are only finished, only completely broken, beyond repair; when you think you are, when you say you are."

You don't have to make a sound, for your voice to be loud.
Those who scream
only want to be heard
But, those who speak,
want to be listened to.

Look at these things you carry as you continuously tread on risking it all to love another.
And they you.

Would you collect my promises like drops of water from
April showers?
Or maybe even,
the flowers that come in spring?
Feed them to your own,
while you keep me on a string?
You selfish bastard

I was your Saturday night,
while you, were my Sunday morning.
And that has always been my problem.

"We are reduced the second we look for validation in those who have betrayed our loyalty."

And if it falls right through the cracks of your fingers, and you finally don't feel the weight of its heaviness, let it be.

Find the eyes to see the world differently. I hope you choose to wander.

"Your perception of love,
has it been filled with deception? Why would you let one
ruin the purity of something we stay alive for?"

If I stripped you bare of your worldly objects, tell me, what is left of you?

Don't forget that love is deeper than your skin. It will hold every ounce of you.

The purity of love
will simply hold you.
not restrain you.

"You are
what you do.
Not your words
that lie empty.
Stealing the interlude
of what I offer you."

Don't lie to me,
my presence doesn't just lie in your bed,
I know, I stay, running
inside of your head."

"She sold me stories of how love was cliché, it filled you with promises of more than Saturday nights. How he will leave notes on your doorstep but leave you standing on his. Empty.
She spoke with such a certainty, that for a moment, I almost believed her."

"I want to be absorbed in light.
I want to become it."

I pray you don't find me to be easily understood. What a colorless reality
that would be.

You can meet me here,
or not at all.
I won't chase another heart.
Just to annihilate mine.

I pulled the petals off of each rose you placed in my hands with my teeth.
All with a smile that met my eyes.
I'm done being your garden.

I loved you heavier than my heart could carry.

Why do we miss the embrace of those who never really held us,
beyond touch?
Because of hope.

I wanted it to be you,
you wanted it to be you too,
but you never wanted it to be me.
I'm tired of loving alone.

Sometimes chaos is simply broken promises and empty words.

"The empty space between each word I let them read, were filled with moments that only you could see."

Oh, I'm restless for a heart which too,
is tired of shallow souls
with nothing to give
but their skin.

"The sunlight dances through the trees, releasing their leaves
that have passed until it's time for their next bloom.
I aspire to accept the things
that nature taught us all, so long ago.
Nothing lasts forever,
learn to let it go."

Have you slowed down yet?
Have you sat in that ear piercing silence?
The one that doesn't let you escape reality.
Which you do so well.
Have you felt the unsteadiness,
the one where you must ground yourself before moving forward.
How heavy it is, to see what could be, left with nothing, but reality.

"You only looked for me when I was gone."
While I saw you, everywhere.
In everything.
In everyone."

"Let me unfold these words for you, it's something I pray you come
to understand, it's the moments
in which you hold a life so simple, without materials within your hands. It's the warmth, when the sun meets your face, the way you favor Sunday mornings.
The way they look at you, without saying anything at all. The time you give, despite it all. Maybe even fearing, just how hard you will fall.
These are, the moments you hold, the moments you remember.
The moments, that change you
in all the best ways.
You take them with you,
without attachment,
without anything,
but simplicity.
Purity.
And no amount of materialism that this world could offer me, would ever teach me,
would ever make me fall in love, over and over again with this life, like these moments.
And even if you don't believe in "Meant to be's"
whether it be human connection or even those material things,
I promise you,
it will make you believe
in something."

"There was a moment where I looked at you,
And it occurred to me, just how deep I already was.
Like a ticking time bomb, an hourglass counting
down the seconds, a wave that swallows you whole
before you have a second to catch your breath.
Suddenly, there was no longer a 'before you',
only 'since you'."

A possibility
the slightest hope
I held it gently.
You and I.

You didn't call.
And I don't know why
but it was the moment
I knew I lost you,
and the moment I knew
If I don't close this door
I'd lose me too.

You reached down my throat and uprooted
words that were meant
for my heart alone.
and I kissed
the intimacy with loss, again.
Is something we all know Far too well.

I saw you, for only a moment.
The real you, the one that you're hesitant
to show the world.
Vulnerable, empty, numb.
but still, feeling all of it.
What left you scared?
Your face in my hands,
a clinched jaw, so you didn't ache too loud, swelled eyes that
pierced a fragile heart, burned into my damn memory. And
god, I hope you find it.
Whatever "it" is.
Whoever she is.

You'll come back.
Maybe even when
it's too late.
And I'll be past the way your smile meets your ears, the way
you laugh
to the point of tears.
Beautiful boy,
how you've wasted
so many years,
all because of fear.

I put the flowers away today.
I tucked them safely inside of a book
that I haven't the slightest want to pick up again,
for now at least.
And they broke apart, slightly while doing so.
And as before, a clinched jaw, a heavy chest, while
trying to be gentle, so nothing else breaks anymore,
including me, I'll leave it be.
Safely in my bookshelf, a chapter I don't have the strength
to read anymore, I'll leave it be. I'll leave you be.

I see you with my eyes closed, I see me laying there, exposed.
I see your eyes, the light reflecting your hues of blue.
I see my hands, holding your face
and I feel the emptiness, that came with your space.

I closed my eyes to escape you, but I found you, instead.

I write you into these pages
into the words, that you don't have the strength to read.
So, when they ask about the "almost"
I hope you think of me.

"What is one thing you hope they see, when they look at you?"

I hope they see how much my eyes light up when I'm talking about the things I love the most.

Poetic is what you called me,
As I run my hands through your hair while accepting the newness of your features compared to what I was trying to move on from.
I want to sink my teeth into your skin as you brace yourself for my wave of giving in – temptation.
I want to breathe in that breath that escaped from your tongue as it rolled onto mine.
I want to remember this, I want to relive it when the numbness overflows within my mind, drowning in the reoccurring thoughts of your willingness to let me in, and me you.
I want to feel you, all of you, one more time.

There's that piece inside of my stomach that slightly aches when I think of you. And when I allow myself to think of you ever so briefly, the ache turns into a wave, that then turns into a hurricane. It all comes back; it still swallows me whole. Your absence still drowns me.

And for the first time
in a long time
I no longer yearned
to be anyone else's,
but mine.

It was you,
and it will be you
for a while.

Have you ever looked into the eyes of someone, and for once felt their honesty?
And you knew that they'd hurt you, even if they didn't mean to. But even still, you just wanted to hold them, in all the ways you could, in all the ways you knew how to. Because you've been there, right where they are, and you just wanted to make it better for them. Even though you know you can't, and even though it's not your place to. Logic left, and you stayed when you shouldn't have. To hold that ticking time bomb. Knowing you would be the one
left in shambles
— it gets better, it always does

And though our tides may have changed, I search for your wave in every current.

"Pause"
Remember the moment, you first tasted love?

The tiny particles
the lasting pieces of me.
do you remember
the day you came
the day you left.
the day, I stayed.
a never-ending script
a pen, the paper, the poems.
and you, the words.

Watch me waste time with those who don't even come close.
Watch me fill a void that I should have kept cold, because no one was as warm as you.

What do you say when they ask you about me?

An ocean is what I saw in you, and I've never wanted to inhale such a depth so deeply.
Until I was completely submerged, gasping for air, drowning inside your hands, inside your closed eyes. I never knew submission to a force so strong, until it took all of me. Until you."

I wrote to you, for you
but the world found them instead.
My Ink covered fingers, my eyes to match them, my words, your words.
They took pieces in what they felt within these lines and gave them to their own.
And I'm still sitting in that spot
wondering if you've found them yet.
Wondering if you'll find me, underneath
that oak tree.

I will no longer try,
no longer pry a heart open
that only chooses to beat
for another.

"Your irresistible urge to seek out newness and unfamiliarity, may you always have the courage to find what shakes your soul to its core."

I longed for sunrises,
they always remained full of color, of life.
and sunsets, the last of those remaining hours.

I found you towards my middle, and me your' beginning.
And that was just how it went. You and I, we were always your story.
It was never mine.

"There is magic
in this life,
in this world.
In destinations,
in places that hold more
than what you seek
inside of another's chest."

It was never about searching for another to fill the space that the one before, took with them so abruptly.
Honestly, I was far past that,
I was doing fine.
And then you
you found your way, inside of my
head, inside of my heart.
And for the first time, in a long time,
I let it happen.
And now, I'm searching.
Expect this time, I know what for
and what to leave behind.
And somehow, both are you.

My soul longs for that vast horizon.
And nothing feels certain as I dive head on into it. Whether it be catastrophic, or fulfilling my every desire, I pray it swallows my entirety
and all that I have left.

"Do you still write about me?"

My ear-to-ear smile was reminded of the moments it was forced without reason, because of the person who asked such question.

I wanted to tell him the truth. That I still see him in river bends and passing strangers.

That I look for him in places without any reason, without trying. That somehow, he still finds his way into my sleeping thoughts, and so I wake up to an empty spot. That sitting in that space, after time spent away from him had passed, I still find myself looking at him like I have just met him. That I'm grasping for

time that I know will soon end. Taking in the moments I get, memorizing his face again, like I don't already know it so well, like it's the last time I'll ever see it.

I wish I could tell him, that he is still in my words when it comes to loving another, even if it was one sided but I know he knows.

"No, I had to let you go. And writing about you kept where I only wish you were, instead of where you are."

I lied to you that night,
When you asked me if I was okay,
if I was past you and I.
Had I told you the truth,
you would have disappeared again, probably for good.
I don't know if I should,
but a part of me doesn't know how, how to leave you be.
I have tried,
I have tried my damndest.
And all I see, is me leaving
soon.
Wishing I had told you I was fine Just one more time.
To see your eyes looking back at me.
So, when I'm thousands of miles away,
I want that last memory of you,
to be all that I see.
Not you walking out the door
that you tried to lock behind you before.
But your eyes, your smile,
because I can't bear
to remember you any other way, but the way I fell in love
with you. And that's the part of you,
I choose, it stays
no matter the proximity – 4400 miles

I am attached to nothing anymore, I've never felt more ungrounded.
And yet, I've never been surer of all the things I questioned before,
including myself.
Especially myself.

But what about the ones who cherished it, knowing it could be lost?
The ones who held the hearts of the ones they loved so gently.
The ones who know the depth of love and loss? The ones who realize the rarity of genuine connection?
What about us?

"You begin to believe it after a while. Telling yourself that you won't 'settle, again'. Finding your
way back to this, back to me, when your head is flooded with pieces of what I do to you. Drowning in your subconscious that makes itself known far too often. Is it lonely knowing that all of you will never be fully satisfied with the mirage you paint inside of your mind every day? I expected more from a man who is used to playing games for a living, but then again, maybe that's exactly what I shouldn't."

And here you are, convenience wins.

"It will take some time,"
You said as you brushed the hair from my eye.
It's been months, and time hasn't yet moved for me. Void filled spaces with another, that make me feel emptier than before I knew what life was like, before you.
What is time when the world around me moves with it, yet I'm still stuck in that moment?
Brief, yes. But it took all of me, all that I had left, when I already didn't have much since beginning again.
How will you remember me when your time has moved years ahead, and somehow, mine is the same?
Is it still considered remembering when I haven't moved from you inside my own four walls?
Is it still okay, that I'm not ready, to not feel only your hands holding my tiny face towards your own?
Is it still okay, that no matter how much your time moves for you, I still choose you. Even without trying to.
Those warped hours that turn into months, that turn into years.
We call it, "time."
And the fear, that I'll be left with my time standing still, sitting right here.
With an empty chair.

There are streams
and there are oceans
there are mountains
and there are hills
there are those
and there is
you.

Reaching for you was like a reoccurring dream that I couldn't shake.
My arms extended, for what seemed like miles on end.
Inside the ear-piercing chaos.
For months, it didn't stop.
It haunts me, the time
I lost holding onto you.
The passing of hours,
I wish it wasn't so,
but here I sit,
staring at that tree
planted outside my window.

I saw my life as it was, full, yet empty. Waiting for me to fill more of its pages with my own promises. And as did you, for your own. We met in our own in-between, and you left before we even started.

I have measured my life in such time, with a set of eyes, that
are only but my own.
And despite all I know,
there is yet, much room still to grow, my fondest lesson is
this, "Nothing happens twice."
Time will alter it all, as it has done since
the beginning. And I promise you,
there is more strength in being fragile,
than in being aware of those two lessons alone.
Because I promise you,
nothing happens twice.

"One day you will look back at the days you teetered on living and just barely surviving. You haven't yet realized just how much you've grown."

They were purple.
The flowers you placed inside my palms.
I looked for them on that mountain again.
And all I found, were weeds
— butterflies and memories

Your name sits softly in the back of my throat. I haven't the strength to speak it since the day I left.

"What made you fall in love with him?"
That question slammed into me harder than I ever imagined it would, but I suppose I never really imagined being asked that question aloud, by an outsider.

I had to catch my breath, find the right words within my head, and make sure they came out right.
"He was easy to fall into. Some days I really wondered if I was in love with him or if I simply just loved him, nothing deeper. I was so lost at the time, and I wasn't looking for anyone or anything. He came out of nowhere, when I was at my most vulnerable. He made laugh, smile, and talk about things I loved again. I loved who I was when he was around. I didn't know I was until later, after he was gone, and we had parted ways. I was driving down the road, and I came upon a stop sign. It was close to a spot where we had sat in his car and talked a while about some in-depth topics. I pulled into the spot where we had parked, and I let myself remember him for the first time in months. The first thought that hit me was how he grabbed my face and kissed me out of nowhere while we were sitting there. It was down pouring outside, and we were waiting
around for our takeout to be ready. I had been talking about something that made me laugh and I was mid-sentence when he grabbed me. I can still see it so vividly, see him so vividly. He had so much emotion behind that kiss, he let the rawness of how he felt slip through his fingers faster than he could catch them. I had to shut my eyes, come back to reality after that memory. And when I did, I realized I was crying, but I was smiling.
It was that moment.

I knew it back then, sitting in that spot with him, but when he left, when I left, I felt such an absence. I didn't even know he held such a space in me. Sometimes I hate myself for letting him, but then I remember a conversation we had not long after meeting. He told me, "We don't choose who we fall in love with, but we do choose who we spend our time with."
He chose differently, as did I. But sometimes, some days, I let myself remember his eyes, the way they matched my own. His smile. The long conversations about everything and nothing. That's when I'm reminded that I loved him, and I never told anyone that out loud, I never told him how I loved his eyes so much. I never told myself, that I loved him, until right now.

I had to leave.
Fucking disappear.
Run away from this place
from you.
But in the end,
all I found were wrong turns
and locked doors.
Which I had the keys to,
But they were not yours.

What was his name?
The one you just felt,
in the back of your throat,
in the clenching of your jaw?"

My mind is a loaded gun,
colliding with its own shots,
and still you ask if I'm okay.

There is no one.
Only the thought of, "who?"
Who am I searching for?
It's no longer, you
as a whole, maybe just pieces of you
in others.
So, what have I learned, in the years of true solitude?
What have I learned, lying naked beside someone who only knows my skin?
That a lot of love, a lot of truth, a lot of transparency, will get you so much further, then a closed soul.
That nothing will make you feel less, than empty
passion.
That, genuine connection, is a rarity. And when you find it, you hold it gently.
That being honest, and raw, is something that not a lot of humans know how to take, but when they see it, when they feel it, they will remember who taught them such a beautiful lesson. They will remember you, your heart.
That being truly alone, is a balancing act of your highest, yet lowest, self.
I have learned, I have learned, I have learned, and thankfully I am still, learning.
So, whomever decides to stumble along the path that I have walked thus far, please know how warming, how thankful, I am to finally meet you.
A letter to you, a letter to your subconscious.

I can't concentrate
I can't focus
my throat burns from the unsaid
my fingers ache from writing on endless
paper trails of old recipes and notebook paper that I dug up from my backpack.
But it's not coming out like I want it to, like I need it to.
It's still heavy god dammit.
It's still heavy.

I packed up what little I had to my name.
I put it in a storage building.
It barley took up any space
I stood there,
white paint covered hands
white paint covered jeans
I locked it. I haven't been back since.

I stare blankly into the creases of the sidewalk.
My body facing the sky, head to the right.
I counted each car that passed by without looking. The distant humming
that turned into quick passing's.
If lie here long enough,
maybe I can drown out the noise,
inside of my head.

I'm tired.
My head is just lifted enough to do what needs to be done.
My body facing inward, unsure of the outside
worlds next move, so I bend with it freely. Hoping it's
gentle.
My eyes are open, but to the ones who see past the front, the very few who see me clearly, they see the exhaustion. I can deal just fine with the physical wearing down of tired, it's the mental tired that can't hide. That's the one that makes itself known to the world around me.
And I don't know how to fake it anymore. I don't know how to open my eyes without the light blinding what vision I have left.
But maybe that's what I need.

The daylight claimed you, and I watched you go.
There isn't a day that has passed,
where I don't relive the moment
I knew and know.

I love you, I loved you.

Sometimes I wonder if it's me you really saw standing in
front of you
unbuttoning my torn to shit jeans
the girl who loved too hard.
but everyone she met, bored her.
A woman knows when you don't see her.
A woman knows a man from a boy.
You were a boy.
And I was a woman.
who knew what she wanted.
So, there we were.
Wishing we were both another.
Distracting each other.

I went alone.
Count it with me.
Twenty years
I went alone
six of them still innocent.
Twenty years I went alone
six of them still naive.
Twenty years I wandered into solitude
six of them still curious.
Twenty years I looked in the wrong places
six of them I slept soundly.
Twenty years I dreamed of leaving
six of them I knew peace.
Twenty years I thought I had it figured out
six of them I knew stability.
Twenty years.
six of them, I knew nothing.
Twenty-six years, I learned that six of them, Were enough to remember.
All of it.
— I was six when you left.

Do you want to know what it's like
to rearrange your life
to meet the acceptance
of those around you?
To hide your voice
though you're not given a choice?
Do you want to know what it's like
through all the slaughtering words,
the ones that gaslight?
To let your tongue roll how it pleases.
To look him in the eyes, and fly regardless from a boy who
should be a man,
And chooses to be heartless.

I don't know what it's like
my tongue and heart stay tongue tied
when it comes to such territory
and I had higher hopes for this story.
But you will do as you have done before,
you'll speak without thinking,
you'll let me walk through that door.
without a goodbye, without an apology.
And you stay wondering why, my trust with
you stays wobbly.

Do you think it was coincidence? The way you found me back then?
When I was just learning to stand up again? When you were hope, and I was lost?
Do you still remember how it felt, to risk it all, given the cost?
And when I let you help me up, when I found steady ground,
I turned to see you leaving, after I tried my damndest to not be found.
And I shut my eyes, because I simply couldn't bare it.
I couldn't stand to see you go, I couldn't watch you walk away.
So, I shut my blinds,

and dreamed of beging you to stay.

The first time we spent time together we drove around aimlessly for hours.
We laughed nervously trying to lift the anxiety of things we held dear to our own hearts. Talked about life, how it kept tripping us up, Meanwhile, all we were trying to do was keep up.
You didn't yet know it, and neither did I. But that was the day I knew I'd love you,
Without trying. Without looking. Effortlessly.
I still choose you. I have since that day.
— nine hundred and thirteen days

Little post it notes, I have doodled for hours. I save them, so I don't waste more paper, kill more trees as I let my hand run that pen free. I can't even do the mindless without worrying if I'm doing this all wrong.
Colored sheets of black and white

"My darling,
if a billion and one
adored you like I,
please know it was me.
The one alongside the billions, the one who counted
your eyelashes
as you slept so soundly.
The one who saw your eyes
light up on the mountains that day.
The one I always run too,
when the suns been away.
So, please know it was me,
alongside the billions.
The one who counted
each second with you
as so precious,
as you slept
so soundly."

Do you think Athena knew
that she would be worshipped for centuries?
Looked upon by women who never feared the fire.
Who never feared war.
Looked down upon by those who call themselves, "men?"
Until they saw her armor.
Do you think she knew that there would come a time that the earth shook when her name was spoken? Immune to romance. Yet, those who knew her fell desperately.
Do you think she knew?
Do you think she gave a fuck?

I flinch when I drive those backroads now. I didn't even realize I was tripping, sinking, into the broken concrete back then, until I drove over them again. The aftermath of surviving, instead of living, is a tightrope of finding balance once coming across a paved road again. I take the interstate now.

A garden;
we planted our own,
all those years ago.
It bloomed slowly,
you are the only one
who really knows me.
Winter came, our garden died. And I, cried and cried,
praying my tears
would bring it back to life.
Spring finally sprung,
and you found me sitting
alongside our garden,
planting, digging.

"There is a house,
on the backside of the west side
and when I lived downtown, the days that I needed to disassociate I would go for a drive straight to
this house, just to marvel at her character.
Old, whitewashed brick, a roof that was brownish from moss and its rounded edges, vines and ivy that have made their home inside the cracks and crevices. Windows that showed her almost entirely, a rounded red door that sits to her left tiredly.
She is old, she seems empty, so I feel comfortable staring at her years, wondering who made her theirs. The seasons changed, for eighteen months I watched the leaves turn its change. I watched the snow lay untouched, along with its house.
And one day it happened, someone new came along. They painted her door, replaced her roof with sharper edges, windows now drawn, ivy and vines torn from there crevice. I know they think they are doing what's better, but I'll miss the way she aged with the weather. The way someone many years ago, loved her red door and how I would despise to tell them that it is now black. It was never even mine, and how I would do anything to have it go back.
I still drive by, just to see how she's doing. I wonder if she too, misses the way she was growing. I wonder if it hurt her knowing, that they saw her years of roots as decomposing."

Even when I think of the dark, the winter shadows that enfold my heart, it is here, that I reach you the most, all of you.
Seasonal depression.

Do you look for me there? On that park bench.
do you look to see if my blinds are pulled, me sitting on that off-white colored couch with a three hour old coffee?
Do you grip the steering wheel harder when you pass that old dirt road?
The one we took on a late drive, and you asked to kiss me.
Do you stare at the spot I once sat when you made me macaroni and cheese at four a.m. after you called me because you couldn't bear to be alone?
Do you still have my letters? Or did you throw them away? Burn them so you'd forget,
so, you wouldn't go looking for them.
Do you still get too drunk to pretend you're okay?
I hope you're doing better, I hope you remember me this way. I hope you know it's almost my time to leave.
I hope you know, how much you meant to me.

Maybe you deserved better. Maybe I did too.

"There are hearts that you will meet, that you'll hold close enough to your soul that you can feel the heat burn inside of your thighs. They will excite your insides; make you jump with anticipation. There are hearts that you will meet that will hold you closer than you them, and you will adore their intentions. Give them a book, they will remember a page, maybe two, but forget the title of the book itself. But there is a heart that you will meet, that will grow with your own. They will excite you even deeper than your skin, they will reach bone. They will buy the book themselves, read every page, and recite the lines they too have lived.

They will run their finger across the curve of your jaw, hold you up when you've fallen to pieces. They will get lost with you in the woods, two thousand miles away from all you both know. Remember what you love the most. And for the first time, in a long time, you will sleep soundly. You will understand a depth you never knew that such an intimacy now runs through your vines. Right through skin, right through bone, right to what matters the most."

Does that turn you on?
Half-naked, bare skin, exposing everything she has to offer?
Do you touch yourself to her?
Do you feel shame after?
You haven't the slightest clue, do you?
How it makes me feel, to know how quick you fall into a temptation without fucking hesitation?
My shame runs deeper, my shame comes from within.
Knowing I gave it all to a boy with a damn mind so paper thin.

It happens like that. Just like that.

One minute you're picking yourself up, you're rummaging through old photos, books, letters, and 'I love you's. You wipe the dust off, and you're right back there. In those moments that you've hidden in a little brown box, on the top shelf of a spare closet that you only use for things you try to hide away from open spaces. Sitting in the doorway of that closet, remembering former reality. And just like that, you're a mirror. With reflections, of blurry views that were once you. That were once us.

"Why must we realize the fragility of life only after we are forced to swallow its hardest lesson. Everything must end, yes, but please remember, only after it's lived."

I wanted Brooklyn NY,
in the middle of fall.
Alone,
a place I have never had a desire to see, until I knew myself better.
I wanted one thirty p.m. coffee with latte art glazed over the top, just barely tipping the sides but not spilling over.
An old, recycled notebook with blank pages and a pen that glides easily.
I wanted to chase down a taxi for the first time and pretend like I knew where the hell I was going.
I wanted a bookstore that smelled of new, but only kept classics hidden within its shelves.
I wanted to sit alone, in a city that was too big for me. Too fast, too crowded, too busy.
I wanted to be alone with my own. I wanted this more than a mountain at dawn, since I was twenty-four. And I still tell myself each spring that its fall will be the one, because I refuse to want Brooklyn in the summer.
And when I've spent my time, I'll head back to those mountains, to my oceans knowing exactly why I fucking adore it more than any place I've ever been told to love more.

It's been ten years,
I want to know, "what would you tell her? What would you tell the young girl, who only dreamed of mountains when she knows just rolling hills? Would you tell her that she gets married too young, and it fails not long after? That she loses a child, after just hearing its heartbeat, on the bathroom floor of the first place that she called home? So now, "home" feels cursed. That she learns to write again, after being silent for five years, but this time she lets the world read it.
That she gives birth to a beautiful blonde headed boy with blue eyes, who reminds her every damn day, that life is worth the moments that you think you can't crawl out of. Because it makes you more grateful for what you do have.
Would you tell her that she travels across the
country, to a place she's been in love with from only seeing pictures. That she sees her whales for the first time in their natural habitat, and she sobs tears of joy?
Would you tell her that love hurts her again, but she writes a book about it and that book finds its way into the hands of others across the world?
Would you tell that young girl, itching to get out of all she knows?
Or would you let her feel it all. Without warning.
Without sugar coating.
Let it break her into someone new. Let it humble her. Let it lead her to work harder. Appreciate deeper. Love unconditionally.
So, tell me,
would you tell her?

The dust collected on the windowsill. I didn't have the capacity to clean it off back then. My plants wilted, a few died. I remember sitting in the middle of the cold hardwood floor, staring at a white wall. A million things to say, but nothing escaped my lips.
My tears felt frozen inside of my eyes, they couldn't leave, they wouldn't leave. Cars outside my window sounded like a distant hum, the heater was too loud,
I couldn't hear the birds. But it was never loud enough to block out the pounding rain. I still think about setting it on fire, that God damn apartment. That empty, dark hallway. A bed that was always cold. A writing desk that collected dust and dried up wildflowers. A single plant that stayed living with
me, and even now, living in my new home. Sometimes it's the smallest things that stay. Whether it be the moments that become memories, or the life that seemed unsteady. It stays, living inside of you, making its place into something new. Again.

It was mid-September,
my favorite time of the year.
A cracked windowpane that looked over to the park.
I can still hear the children playing in that.
muffled echo.
And the park bench.
That fucking park bench.
It has been years now, not just one.
I don't go to that park any more.
But I passed it yesterday for the first time since I left my keys to that old apartment under the mat, and my lungs felt heavy.
Even now.
The same song on repeat that still brings me to my knees.
That golden autumn sun hit my eyes,
my hand hard gripped the steering wheel,
and suddenly it consumed me all over again.
Maybe some things will never change.
Maybe your memory will always ache.
Maybe, some things will live inside us forever.

They said I'd be better by now.
You said I'd be better by now.

The skin I burned
holding on to a rope so paper thin.
slipping through my cracked hands.
The voice that choked when I tried to tell you.
That even at twenty-six, I still cry for you,
for what was lost.
I think the worst loss of all
is a death of someone still breathing.
Living without you,
leaning how to,
has me thinking of old memories
That are burned inside of my eyes.
When did you decide,
that it was better this way?

If I could rewind time, I would sit with you just a little longer.

And you're still lying on the cracked concrete.
Eyes to the sky, tears that burn your cheek that fall on to that concrete
your throat burns from keeping the gasps inside.
It started a whisper,
it turned into a scream.
Looking for a cloud to cover the suns light
in a clear blue sky.

You're looking for a reason to cry,
aren't you?

Elements of the universe,
broken into tiny fragments,
my fingers running through your red hair
bright eyed, full on a love, a lust, that burned the inside of my thighs.
Shadows that moved like the ocean.
Steady, until the rain.
You've memorized every piece of me,
my pale skin, that I learned to love.
And I begged for your hand to leave an imprint on my throat.
Your mouth that sets the waves in motion,
my god, give me all of you.
Lips that somehow silenced the world around me,
begging for your ridge surface.
A place where we both lose reality,
besides the elements of our own world.
The tiny fragments that made us one.
A universe inside me.

"He loved it, didn't he?
The way you made him feel about himself.
And you knew he never truly loved you, or what you had to offer.
He loved who he was when he was with you.
You put him on a pedestal, and he'd never seen the world from up there.
Wrapping himself in what words that spilled out of your mouth to make him feel safe.
To make him feel anything but what you've felt yourself.
You made him feel like the man he truly wanted to be deep down, without him doing the work himself.
But he wasn't a man.
He was a damaged boy,
who used every piece of you.
Your body, your fucking universe of a mind.
Your heart that knows no boundaries when it comes to making someone feel more love than what you had to offer.

And he knew that, didn't he?"

I want mountains that tower over clouds.
An ocean that kisses the horizon,
the sun that rises from its depth.
I want to stand underneath a waterfall.
Feeling the water hit my naked body with such a force, it takes my breath away.
I want to climb the mountain that I love so fiercely.
The way she dominates the west coast.

He held my hand,
when the other left.
Tucked me into bed
never a set time.
Slept on single mattress
a few boxes on the floor.
Flipping houses,
so we'd have more.
Sits in his recliner,
until I fall asleep.
Sits me on his shoulders,
so I could see.
But somehow, now
how it has changed.
I can't remember the last time
he even said my name.
I looked for something in others,
Made a mess of my youth.
All because I was looking
for you.

Finger printed windows
stained glass with streaks of falling rain.
Shadows on my bedroom floor.
Love notes scribbled on a paper
torn from its seams.
I find you here,
there, and everywhere
In between.

Love lives in my chest without planting its seed. I thought I'd let it grow easily. But the more I see, the more I feel, the more I come to understand
my own heart.
And I am starting to realize as much as I ache to let it grow, the more terrified I am to just let it go.
Maybe this is where I find safety.
Poems for them to fold into their old, beaten-up wallets.
Writing about a love that climbs up and out of my throat into the hands of those
brave enough to carry it.
I'll be the voice; you be the hero.
Tell me it's as beautiful,
as it seems.

You look for me in small minds.
In skin that has been seen and touched by anyone who gives it attention.
You fill the void with her paper-thin heart.
While your eyes follow my every move from across the room.
Does that piece in the pit of your stomach still get anxious, when you think about us?
Do you drive by my favorite coffee shop and do your damndest to not look?
The nights you decide to sleep alone, you toss and turn.
You've yet to open your curtains since I told you I prefer the suns light instead.
My name is spoke and you still clench your jaw, keeping your eyes fixed head on.
Tell me, I want to know.

You trace your finger down my naked spine, and my body arches with it.
And the way your eyes lock into mine while your head is in between my legs.
A kinetic force, I've only ever felt with you.
Tell me you'll stay.

I keep telling myself stories in my head.
That one day, my heart would end up in gentle hands.
Where I'd walk an overgrown path of wildflowers and braided ivy with someone whose smile is somehow more contagious than my own desire for solitude.
That I can let my shoulders fall with grace and unravel the knots they made from years of worry.
That when love decides to visit again, they will remember that my favorite flower is a peony, that I prefer my coffee with coconut milk and three sugars.
That I write my best after a few drinks, that my favorite place in this entire world is on a mountain in the Pacific North West, that my favorite color changes from black, to yellow, to an ocean blue.
And the letters that I've wrote,
that I slipped into back porch doors
taught me what love wasn't,
so I could make space,
for what love was.